THE BIBLE:

THE BIG PICTURE

by John and Lori Verstegen

2nd Edition
Berean Bible Ministries
P.O. Box 81
San Juan Capistrano, CA 92693

www.helpersofyourjoy.com
(949) 364-3138 / (949) 347-7635

A NOTE

This book was written with the hope that it will help Christians better understand and enjoy the Bible, for it is through the written word of God that we come to truly know and love the living Word of God. Nothing is more blessed than to more fully know our Lord and Saviour Jesus Christ and all the many blessings that are ours "in Him."

As you read, we pray that you will be like the noble Bereans who "received the word with all readiness of mind, and searched the scriptures daily, whether those things were so" (Acts 17:11). As you read, ask, "For what saith the scripture?" (Romans 4:3), and look up each verse referenced. You will be amazed at how wonderfully the verses in the Bible, like pieces of a puzzle, fit together to reveal God's marvelous two-fold plan and purpose for the heaven and the earth in Christ Jesus.

Remember, Scripture alone is our final authority and source of truth. It is "the word of God, which effectually worketh also in you that believe" (I Thessalonians 2:13).

Please do also note that all verses used in this book are from the King James Version of the Bible. We strongly urge you to use the KJV when "searching the scriptures" as the modern versions have made many changes to the text. (If you would like a simple brochure comparing the translations, please visit our website: www.helpersofyourjoy.com.)

In some of the verses quoted, we have placed words in bold letters for emphasis. The bolding is ours. It is not in the KJV. However, words that appear in italics are words that are italicized in the KJV.

TABLE OF CONTENTS

MID-ACTS THROUGH PAUL'S EPISTLES
PROPHECY INTERRUPTED:
GOD'S PLAN TO RESTORE THE HEAVENS REVEALED:
THE CHURCH, THE BODY OF CHRIST ("The Mystery")

HEBREWS THROUGH REVELATION
PROPHECY RESUMES FULFILLMENT

APPENDIX

INTRODUCTION

The Bible (scripture) is God's eternal, inspired word. Psalm 119:89 and Daniel 10:21[1] teach that it was settled in heaven before it was ever written on earth. God's word guides all that God does. By it "the worlds were framed" (Hebrews 11:3), and in it is God's offer of eternal life to those who will believe it.

God's word is his revelation to us of himself. We know God through his word. The central person of the Bible is the Lord Jesus Christ, the living Word of God (John 1:1). He is pictured in some way in every one of its books. Hebrews 10:7 says, "in the volume of the book it is written of me." He is the seed of the woman, the great high priest, the Passover lamb, the kinsman redeemer, the rock of salvation, the chief cornerstone, the seed of David, the great "I AM," the Son of God, the Head of the church, and so much more. Jesus Christ is also rightfully "the blessed and only Potentate, the King of kings, and Lord of lords" of all things—both in heaven and on earth (I Timothy 6:15; Colossians 1:16).

However, since Lucifer's fall, there has been rebellion in *both* realms of God's kingdom. The Bible reveals God's two-fold plan to end the rebellion, "that at the name of Jesus every knee should bow, of *things* in heaven and *things* in earth, and *things* under the earth . . ." (Philippians 2:10).

Through Israel—the nation God created and will one day redeem— he will reclaim the earth. Through "the body of Christ"—the church he is currently creating[2]—he will reclaim the heavenly places. Thus, "in the dispensation of the fullness of times" he will "gather together in one **all things in Christ, both which are in heaven, and which are on earth.**"[3] This is the eternal purpose and two-fold plan of God revealed in the Bible. *The Bible: The Big Picture* was written to help you see how and where *you* fit into the outworking of this plan.

---

1. *An angel told Daniel that he would show him "that which **is** noted in the scripture of truth." Daniel 11 was already written in heaven before Daniel wrote it down on earth!*
2. *I Corinthians 12:27; Colossians 1:24-25*
3. *Ephesians 1:10*

"RIGHTLY DIVIDING THE WORD OF TRUTH"

Seeing how and where *you* fit into the outworking of God's plan is vital because while all the Bible is *for* us, it is not all *to* us nor is it all *about* us. We cannot open the Bible and apply any and all verses to ourselves. For example, many passages command animal sacrifices. Obviously, no true Christian would teach that we should offer animal sacrifices today. We must distinguish between verses that apply *today* and verses that do not. We must "rightly divide the word of truth" (II Timothy 2:15 KJV). Understanding "the big picture," and God's two-fold plan, will help us do this.

SALVATION

In no other area is "rightly dividing" more important than it is in understanding how to be saved from hell and stand completely forgiven and justified before a holy God. From cover to cover, the Bible teaches that salvation is by faith in God's word, for "without faith it is impossible to please him" (Hebrews 11:6), and ". . . faith cometh by hearing, and hearing by the word of God" (Romans 10:17). Saving faith is always a positive response to God's revealed word. However, God's *revealed* word has not always been the same in every age. So, it is imperative that you know what his word is TO YOU!

"Time Past" (Eph. 2:11)

The shed blood of Christ is the payment for the sins of all men of all ages. No one, in any age, could ever be saved except by the shed blood of Christ. However, in time past, prior to the cross, people did not know this. God had not yet revealed it, so their faith had to be placed in God's revealed word to them *at that time*. When it was, God looked ahead to the cross in order to forgive their sins (Romans 3:25). According to Hebrews 11, by faith Abel offered a sacrifice, Noah prepared an ark, Abraham left his land and offered up Isaac, and Moses forsook Egypt.

To Israel, God gave his law. Clearly, Israelites could not have had true faith in God and at the same time refuse to offer the sacrifices commanded in the law. The sacrifices did not save them, but they were the evidence of their faith in God's revealed word to them. In time past, then, faith was manifest by works.

"But Now" (Romans 3:21)

Today, though, God's Word tells us that we are not under the law, but under grace (Romans 6:14). God has revealed to us who live after the cross that Christ has done all the work necessary to save us — He shed his blood as the full payment for all of our sins, died, and rose again as proof that God has accepted the payment (Romans 3:21-28 and 4:25).

Today God tells *us* to STOP WORKING for salvation and trust in the work of his son for our justification:

> "But to him that **worketh not**, but **believeth on him** that justifieth the ungodly, his faith is counted for righteousness" (Romans 4:5).

True faith today, then, will be manifest by resting in the shed blood of Christ, and that *alone*, for justification. Adding works of any kind (water baptism, committing your life to Christ, walking an aisle, keeping the law, repeated confession of sins . . .) to the work of Christ *in order to obtain forgiveness or salvation* is a denial that HIS work is enough. It is not faith in God's good news in this age of grace.

"Ages to Come"

What about in the future? This age of grace will not last forever. One day the church, the body of Christ, will be taken home to heaven, and God will have another message for the world — one that will again require works, such as not taking the mark of the beast (Revelation 14:9-12). But this will be much clearer after reading *The Bible — The Big Picture*.

CREATION: BY AND FOR CHRIST

The Bible begins by telling us that God created the heaven and the earth. Note that throughout the Bible these two realms are distinct. When speaking of creation, God does not use the word "universe" but, instead, specifies "the heaven and the earth."[1]

We learn that God created all things in heaven and on earth by and for his son, the Lord Jesus Christ. The "all things" include "thrones, dominions, principalities, and powers."[2] Jesus Christ was, and is, to be "the blessed and only Potentate, the King of kings, and Lord of lords" over all of creation, both in heaven and earth.[3]

Even in the eternal state, the distinction between heaven and earth will remain in "a new heaven and a new earth."[4]

SEARCH THE SCRIPTURES

1. *Genesis 1:1; Ephesians 3:15*
2. *Colossians 1:16*
3. *I Timothy 6:15; Philippians 2:10-11; Ephesians 1:10; Colossians 1:16-20*
4. *Revelation 21:1; Isaiah 65:17; II Peter 3:13*

LUCIFER: "I WILL"

However, one of God's creatures did not like God's plan. His name was Lucifer. Lucifer was "the anointed cherub that covereth."[1] He was created to lead the angelic host in song and praise to God. He was covered with beautiful stones that reflected the glory of God throughout the heavens.[2] His position was higher than any other created being, but Lucifer was not satisfied. He wanted to be "like the most High."[3]

Genesis 14:19 and 22 (KJV) define the title, "the most high God," as the title that speaks of God being "the possessor of heaven and earth." Satan wanted to possess heaven and earth. His pride caused his fall, and he became Satan, the Devil.

SEARCH THE SCRIPTURES

1. *Ezekiel 28:14*
2. *Ezekiel 28: 13*
3. *Isaiah 14: 12-15*

REBELLION IN HEAVEN

Since his fall, Satan's plan has been to take control of all creation. He led a rebellion in heaven and many angels followed him.[1] God says the heavens are unclean in his sight.[2] In fact, God originally prepared hell for these fallen angels.[3]

Since God knew beforehand that Lucifer would rebel, he had a plan to one day cleanse the heavens and restore them to the headship of the Lord Jesus Christ. However, he kept his plan to do so secret, so that Satan and his princes would not know it.[4] God did not reveal his plan to restore the *heavenly places* anywhere in the Old Testament, so we will not discover it until much later in the Bible.

For now, just remember that God did have a plan to regain complete control of the heavenly places, but he would only make it known in due time.

SEARCH THE SCRIPTURES

1. *Revelation 12:9; Job 4:18; Eph. 6:12*
2. *Job 15:15*
3. *Matthew 25:41*
4. *I Corinthians 2:7-8; Eph. 3:9-10*

REBELLION ON EARTH

When God created Adam and Eve, he instructed them to have dominion over the earth. Satan sought to continue his rebellion there. God had given Adam one simple command: "... of the tree of the knowledge of good and evil, thou shalt not eat of it: for in the day that thou eatest thereof thou shalt surely die."[1] Satan, the serpent, questioned God's word by asking, "Yea, hath God said ... ?"[2] Then he challenged God's word by lying, "Ye shall not surely die."[3]

Instead of trusting God's word, Adam and Eve ate of the fruit. Thus, they brought sin and death into the world, and the earth was placed under a curse.[4] Because of this, Satan was able to take dominion of the earth from Adam.[5]

But this did not take God by surprise, either. Just as God had a plan to take back the heavens, he had a plan to take back the earth. However, he *did* begin to reveal his plan for *the earth*, little by little, right from the beginning of the world.[6] This is what we read about in the Old Testament.

The Old Testament covenants and prophecies reveal God's eternal plans *for the earth*.

SEARCH THE SCRIPTURES

1. *Genesis 2:17*
2. *Genesis 3:1*
3. *Genesis 3:4*
4. *Genesis 3:16-19; Romans 5:12*
5. *Luke 4:5-6; John 14:30; 2 Corinthians 4:4*
6. *Luke 1:70; Acts 3:21*

THE OLD TESTAMENT

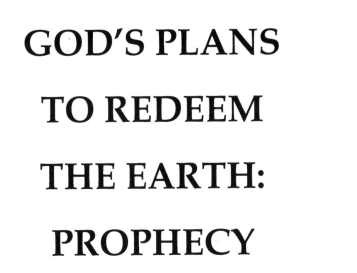

GOD'S PLANS
TO REDEEM
THE EARTH:
PROPHECY

THE SEED OF THE WOMAN

At the fall of man, God told the serpent (Satan) that his seed would bruise the heel of the seed of the woman, but her seed (meaning a man, not an angel) would eventually bruise his head.[1] We now know, from further revelation in God's word, that the seed of the woman is Jesus Christ, who will one day destroy Satan.

But Jesus Christ did not come right away. God let men multiply on the earth. As they did, Satan and his angels attempted to contaminate the human race in order to prevent the pure seed of the woman from coming.[2]

By Genesis 6, Satan had infected the human race so completely that only one man was "perfect in his generations."[3] So, God sent a flood to destroy all of mankind except for Noah and his family. From Noah's family the earth was repopulated,[4] and the promised seed of the woman would eventually be born.

SEARCH THE SCRIPTURES

1. Genesis 3:15
2. Genesis 6:1-4
3. Genesis 6:9
4. Genesis 9:19

THE ABRAHAMIC COVENANT

As men multiplied on the earth again, they soon became captive to Satan's idolatry and rebellion. God had told them to spread over all the earth; instead, "they said, Go to, let us build us a city and a tower, whose top *may reach* unto heaven; and let us make us a name lest we be scattered abroad upon the face of the whole earth" (Genesis 11:4).

So God confused their languages, and the earth became divided into nations. God "gave them up" and "gave them over to a reprobate mind."[1]

At this point, God revealed a little more about his plan to regain the earth: he would make his **own special nation** from a man named Abram (Abraham). He would use this nation to bless all the other nations.[2] His nation would dwell in a special land, Canaan. He told Abraham the borders of the great kingdom his seed would one day have on this earth.[3]

Remember this part of the covenant especially:

THE ABRAHAMIC COVENANT

"I will make of thee a great <u>nation</u>, and I will bless thee, and make thy name great; and thou shalt be a blessing: And I will bless them that bless thee, and curse him that 5curseth thee: and in thee shall all families of the earth be blessed." (Genesis 12:1-3)

SEARCH THE SCRIPTURES

1. *Genesis 11:1-9 with Romans 1:24, 26, 28*
2. *Genesis 12:1-3; 18:18*
3. *Genesis 15:18-21; 17:8*

ISRAEL: GOD'S CHOSEN NATION ON EARTH

God had promised to make a great nation from Abraham's seed, but Abraham and Sarah did not have any children. They were getting older and older. Eventually they were too old to have children. This is when God gave them a miracle child, Isaac. The Abrahamic Covenant was passed to him[1] and then to his son, Jacob.[2]

God changed Jacob's name to Israel, which means "Prince of God." Israel had twelve sons. They became the 12 tribes of Israel. The Abrahamic Covenant was passed to them.[3]

From this point forward, God's nation would be named Israel. People of all other nations were called Gentiles. God made a difference between Israel and the Gentiles and erected what he called "the middle wall of partition" between them.[4]

When God spoke, he spoke to and through Israel. *They were to be his channel of blessing to the world.*

Abraham

⬇

Isaac

⬇

Jacob (Israel)

⬇

The twelve tribes of

ISRAEL

MIDDLE WALL OF PARTITION

GENTILES

"...aliens from the commonwealth of Israel, and strangers from the covenants of promise . . . without God in the world"

(Ephesians 2:12)

SEARCH THE SCRIPTURES

1. *Genesis 17:19,21*
2. *Genesis 28:13-14*
3. *Psalm 105:8-11*
4. *Leviticus 20:24-26; Ephesians 2:11,14*

MOSES: THE DELIVERER

God told Abram (Abraham) that his seed would be strangers in a land that was not their own. They would be afflicted for 400 years. Afterwards, God would deliver them out of bondage.[1] This is indeed what happened.

The sons of Jacob (Israel) became slaves in Egypt. But just as God had promised, after 400 years, he sent a deliverer, Moses, to take his people out of Egypt to their promised land.

Through Moses God worked many great signs and wonders that proved that the earth belonged to him and that the children of Israel were his people. God defeated the gods of the Egyptians,[2] destroyed Pharaoh and his army in the Red Sea, and brought Israel safely out of Egypt. He said that Israel would "be a peculiar treasure unto me above all people: **for all the earth is mine.**"[3]

God's people had gone down to Egypt as a small family, but by the time they exited Egypt they were over a million in number. Their passage through the Red Sea, out of Egypt, was their birth as a nation. God called them his "son" and his "firstborn."[4]

SEARCH THE SCRIPTURES

1. *Genesis 15:13-16*
2. *Exodus 12:12*
3. *Exodus 19:5-6*
4. *Exodus 4:22; Numbers 11:11-12*

THE MOSAIC COVENANT: ISRAEL TO BE A KINGDOM OF PRIESTS

When Israel left Egypt, God was with them. He said, "Ye have seen . . . *how* I bare you on eagles' wings, and brought you unto myself."[1] In the wilderness, he miraculously provided for all their needs. He sent manna (bread from heaven), quail, and water. Their clothes and their shoes did not wear out.[2] God was with them every step of the way, yet the people constantly murmured and lost trust in God. Because of this, it took 40 years for them to enter into their promised land. (The generation of those who doubted God had to die before the rest could enter in.)[3]

Through Moses God gave the people of Israel his law, statutes, and judgments. The purpose of this was to set them apart from all the other people.[4] *They were supposed to be a light and an example to the rest of the nations.*[5]

THE MOSAIC COVENANT

Under the law God said that if Israel obeyed, he would bless them in their land and make them a kingdom of priests and an holy nation.[6]

However, if they disobeyed, God would curse them. He would take them out of their land and scatter them among the nations.[7]

SEARCH THE SCRIPTURES

1. *Exodus 19:4*
2. *Exodus 16:12-15; 15:24-25; 17:6; Deuteronomy 29:5*
3. *Numbers 14:22-23, 28-35*
4. *Leviticus 20:24-26*
5. *Deuteronomy 4:6-8; Psalm 147:19-20*
6. *Exodus 19:5-6; Isaiah 61:6*
7. *Leviticus 26:27-33*

SACRIFICES & FEASTS OF THE LAW:
A PICTURE OF ISRAEL'S REDEMPTION

Because all men are sinful, no one, not even God's people, could keep the law perfectly. So, God gave them a means whereby they could maintain their relationship with him. He instructed them to offer animal sacrifices as an atonement for their sins.[1] When they believed God and offered a sacrifice *by faith,* the blood of the animals *covered* their sins.

Though they did not know it, these sacrifices were a picture of the coming sacrifice of Christ that God looked forward to — the sacrifice that would *completely take away* their sins forever.[2]

Under the law, God also gave Israel feast days to observe. Three times a year all Israelite men were to go before the Lord to keep these feasts:[3]

- ❖ **Unleavened Bread** (with Passover & Firstfruits)[4]

- ❖ **Feast of Harvest**
  (Also called Pentecost. It was 50 days later.)[5]

- ❖ **Feast of Ingathering**
  (Trumpets, Day of Atonement, Tabernacles)[6]

These feasts picture how God will eventually redeem his people and bring them into their promised land eternally. They picture real events that we will read about later: the crucifixion and resurrection of Christ, Pentecost, the gathering of the faithful of Israel, the Second Coming of Christ, and the establishment of the kingdom on earth.[7]

SEARCH THE SCRIPTURES

1. *Leviticus 1:1-4*
2. *Romans 3:25; Hebrews 9:24-10:18*
3. *Exodus 23:14-17*
4. *Exodus 23:15; Leviticus 23: 1-14*
5. *Exodus 23:16a; Lev. 23: 15-22*
6. *Exodus 23:16b; Lev. 23:23-44*
7. *Colossians 2:16-17*

THE DAVIDIC COVENANT:
A THRONE & KINGDOM ON EARTH FOREVER

When Israel first entered their promised land, they went through periods of obedience and disobedience. Eventually, though, a great king arose who served God. His name was David. Under David, Israel had a mighty kingdom, and God made a special promise to him.

To David, God revealed a little more about his plan to regain the earth. He promised that one day David's seed, who will also be *God's son,* will sit on *David's throne in Jerusalem* and *rule over Israel forever.* Once this happens, Israel will dwell in the *land* promised to Abraham *forever,* and God's kingdom will be established on the earth *forever.*[1]

It is important to recognize that the kingdom described in the Davidic Covenant is a literal, physical kingdom to be established upon this earth, just like David's kingdom.

THE DAVIDIC COVENANT

A king from the seed of David (who will also be God's son) will rule over Israel from Jerusalem forever. When he does, the people of Israel will dwell in their own land in peace and safety *forever.*

SEARCH THE SCRIPTURES

1. *2 Samuel 7:10-17*

ISRAEL SCATTERED

David's son Solomon ruled next. His kingdom was a magnificent kingdom. At the height of its glory, it was a picture and type of the kingdom reign of God's son, the Lord Jesus Christ. The entire world heard of its glory, and kings and queens came to see it and honor Solomon.[1]

For most of Solomon's reign, he served God. However, in his later years, he took many wives who led him into idolatry. Because of this, Israel's kingdom was split into two parts: Israel (10 tribes) and Judah (two tribes). [2]

Then, every king in Israel (the northern kingdom, later also called Samaria) led the people into idolatry. So, as God had warned under the law, he took them out of the land by letting the Assyrians conquer them and carry them away.[3]

Later, Judah (the southern kingdom) also went into idolatry and was taken out of their land by the Babylonians. [4]

The people of Israel were now scattered among the Gentiles, out of their land. This was God's judgment upon them for their continual disobedience. It is exactly what he had told them he would do if they did not obey his laws: "I will scatter you among the heathen, and will draw a sword out after you: and your land shall be desolate..."[5]

SEARCH THE SCRIPTURES

1. I Kings 10: 23-25; 2 Chronicles 9:13-14 & 22-24
2. I Kings 11:9-13, 31-39; I Kings 12: 17, 20-24
3. 2 Kings 17:6+;
4. 2 Kings 24:1-16
5. Leviticus 26:33-39

A NEW COVENANT WITH ISRAEL

Israel had failed under the Mosaic Covenant, but God would not forget his promises to Abraham, Isaac, Jacob, and David, which were not dependent upon Israel's obedience.

Through the prophets, God revealed that he would one day "make a new covenant with the house of Israel, and with the house of Judah."[1]

Under the new covenant, God will do in them what they could not do on their own. He said, "I will put my law in their inward parts, and write it in their hearts."

He promised, "a new heart also will I give you [Israel] ... And I will ... cause you to walk in my statutes, and ye shall keep my judgments and do *them*. And ye shall dwell in the land that I gave to your fathers; and ye shall be my people, and I will be your God."[1]

God will one day gather Israelites from everywhere he has scattered them and bring them back into their promised land where they will dwell forever.[2] David's son, who will also be God's son, will be king over them and rule from Jerusalem in a kingdom of perfect righteousness.[3]

A NEW COVENANT

God will do in Israel what they could not do for themselves: He will put his law in their hearts and cause them to do his will. Hence, Israel WILL one day be the light to the Gentiles that God intended them to be—a kingdom of priests. They will bring God's salvation to the world.[4]

SEARCH THE SCRIPTURES

1. *Jeremiah 31:31-34; Ezekiel 36:26-28*
2. *Ezekiel 36:22-28; Ezekiel 37:21-28; Isaiah 11:10-12*
3. *Jeremiah 23:3-8; Ezekiel 37:24-28; Jeremiah 33:15-17*
4. *Isaiah 61:6-9; Isaiah 60:3-5 & 10-16; Zechariah 8:23*

PROPHETS TELL OF ISRAEL'S KINGDOM

The prophets confirmed the promises of the new covenant and gave more details about God's plan to restore the earth to Christ's rule:

- ❖ God will send his son to save his people (Israel) from their enemies and their sins.[1] He will conquer Satan and free his people and his land of him.[2] But he will first suffer and be "cut off" for the sins of his people (Israel).[3]

- ❖ God's son, the seed of David, will set up his kingdom and rule the earth from Jerusalem forever.[4] The curse will be removed from the earth.[5] There will be a great healing of the people.[6]

- ❖ During the kingdom, the people of Israel will be gathered into their land where they will be a kingdom of priests and a light to the Gentiles. Nations who want to be blessed will seek God in Jerusalem and will bless Israel. (The fulfillment of the Abrahamic Covenant.)[7]

- ❖ However, before the kingdom is established, God will purge Israel during a time of chastening called "the time of Jacob's trouble,"[8] more commonly known as the tribulation period. He will destroy the rebels from among Israel, so that only true believers—"the little flock," "the elect," "the righteous," "the remnant"—will enter the kingdom.[9]

SEARCH THE SCRIPTURES

1. *Zacharias summarizes the prophets in Luke 1:67-77*
2. *Isaiah 49: 24-25 with Matt. 12:29*
3. *Isaiah 53:6-12; Psalm 22; Psalm 2*
4. *Isa. 24:23; Jer. 3:17; Zech. 8:3-8; Isa. 9:7; Jer. 33:15-16; Matt. 5:35*
5. *Ezekiel 36:35; Isaiah 11:6-9 & 35:1-2*
6. *Isaiah 35:5-6*
7. *Isa. 11:10-16; Zech. 8:21-23; Isa. 60:12-14; Isa. 62; Isa. 2:2-3*
8. *Jeremiah 30:7*
9. *Malachi 3:2-4; Zechariah 13:8-9; Ezek. 20:37-42; Ezek. 22:18-2*

DANIEL'S TIME SCHEDULE

The prophet Daniel gave a time schedule of the events that will occur prior to the establishment of God's kingdom—the kingdom of heaven upon the earth.[1]

He prophesied that 69 weeks of years (483 years) after "the commandment to restore and to build Jerusalem," Messiah would come.[2] So, once this event happened (Nehemiah 2), those who believed God's word could count the years until Messiah would come. According to Sir Robert Anderson, 483 years after the commandment was given is the very day that Christ rode into Jerusalem on the foal of a donkey.[3]

Daniel had been taken to Babylon when King Nebuchadnezzar's army invaded Judah. The king had a dream that Daniel interpreted. The dream revealed that, beginning with the Babylonian Empire, Gentile kingdoms would rule over Israel *until* Messiah establishes God's kingdom.[4] This era of Gentile domination is called "the times of the Gentiles."[5]

After the last Old Testament prophet wrote, God would not speak again until he would send the prophet to announce the arrival of the Messiah.[6]

SEARCH THE SCRIPTURES

1. *Daniel 2:44; Deuteronomy 11:21*
2. *Daniel 9:25*
3. *Anderson, Sir Robert.* The Coming Prince. *Grand Rapids: Kregel Publications, 1977. Chapter X.*
4. *Daniel 2:36-45*
5. *Luke 21:24*
6. *Amos 8:11-12*

COVENANTS AND PROPHECIES BEGIN TO BE FULFILLED

"THE TIME IS FULFILLED . . . THE KINGDOM OF GOD IS AT HAND"

God was silent for approximately 400 years. Then, right on time, Messiah was born. It is significant that Matthew begins by telling us that Jesus Christ is **"the son of David, the son of Abraham"** because Jesus Christ came to fulfill the Davidic and Abrahamic Covenants.[1]

Remember, in these covenants, God promised to make of Abraham's seed a great nation (Israel) through whom God would bless the world. That nation was to be given a king of the seed of David, who will rule over Israel from Jerusalem forever. In that kingdom, Israel will dwell in her own land in peace and safety forever, ministering to the Gentiles.[2] At the birth of John the Baptist, Zacharias reaffirmed these promises when he prophesied that his son would prepare the way of the Lord. *Please read Luke 1:67-79 carefully.*

When the appointed time arrived, God broke his silence by sending John the Baptist—"the voice of one crying in the wilderness"[3]—to announce the arrival of the Messiah and the "at hand" phase of the kingdom God had promised Israel. John is called the greatest prophet[4] because, as Christ stated, "the law and the prophets *were* **until** John: since that time the kingdom of God is preached."[5]

The law and the prophets before John had proclaimed that the kingdom was coming, but with the arrival of the Messiah, John was sent to announce that the kingdom was AT HAND.[6]

SEARCH THE SCRIPTURES

1. *Matthew 1:1; Romans 15:8; Romans 9:4-5*
2. *See pages 17 & 22; Isa 61:6; Isa 62: 1-3*
3. *Isaiah 40:3; Matthew 3:3*
4. *Luke 7:28*
5. *Luke 16:16*
6. *Matthew 3:2; John 1:6*

JOHN THE BAPTIST: THE FORERUNNER

As prophesied, God sent his messenger, the forerunner, John, to announce *to Israel, "Repent, for the kingdom of heaven is at hand."*[1]

*(It is called "the kingdom of heaven" because it is heavenly in nature. Clearly, it is the kingdom promised to Israel in the Old Testament when the "God of heaven" will establish it upon this earth [Dan. 2:44]. Deut. 11:21 calls it "the days of **heaven upon the earth**.")*

At that time Israel, spiritually, was ruled by the religious traditions of the scribes and Pharisees, who were Satan's pawns.[2] Satan had also filled the land and the nation with his devils because he knew it was time for God's son to claim his land and his people. So, John went outside of Jerusalem, into the wilderness, to separate himself from the apostate nation and to call out a remnant of those who would believe.[3]

Those who responded to John were baptized *"for the remission of sins."*[4] Water baptism separated them from "the generation of vipers" who will be purged out of Israel during "the wrath to come."[5]

Water baptism was also necessary for Israel at that time because, under the law, water washing was required for cleansing those who would serve in the priesthood.[6] Remember, Israel was to be a "kingdom of priests"[7]—God's channel of blessing to the rest of the world—but they had become unclean.

To reach the world, God had to first cleanse and save Israel.

SEARCH THE SCRIPTURES

1. *Matthew 3:2; John 1:31; Malachi 3:1*
2. *Matt. 15:3-9 and Matt. 23 (all); John 8:44*
3. *Matthew 3:1-7*
4. *Mark 1:4; Luke 3:3*
5. *Matt. 3:7; Lk. 7:30; Matt. 23:35-36; Also, see page 25, note 7 & 8*
6. *Exodus 29:4*
7. *Exodus 19:5-6 & Isa 61:6-9*

THE MINISTRY OF CHRIST TO ISRAEL

Jesus Christ was the Son of God, the Messiah, the king promised to Israel in the Old Testament. He preached *to Israel* "the gospel of the kingdom," which Mark 1:14-15 define as this:

> "*The time is fulfilled, and* **the kingdom of God is at hand**... "[1]

Christ was "a minister of the circumcision . . . to confirm the promises *made* unto the fathers."[2] He said very clearly,

> "*I am not sent but* **unto the lost sheep of the house of Israel**."[3]

Christ taught that salvation was through him. Those who believed that he was "the Son of God . . . the King of Israel" would receive eternal life in the kingdom.[4] He also taught obedience to the law given to Israel.[5] Christ went to Israel because Israel was to be the channel of blessing to the Gentiles. Christ came to Israel in order to reach the world through Israel's rise to kingdom glory. The Abrahamic Covenant (page 17) was still in effect. To be blessed, Gentiles had to bless Israel and believe the kingdom gospel. Study the two Gentiles who are blessed in the gospels:

The centurion in Luke 7:2-5 was blessed because he sent elders of the **Jews** to Jesus to ask for the healing of his servant. The Jews told Christ that he was worthy, "**For he loveth our nation, and he hath built us a synagogue.**"

The woman of Canaan in Matthew 15:22-28 did not receive healing for her daughter until she acknowledged that she understood her place as a Gentile under the Abrahamic Covenant. When Christ said to her, "It is not meet to take the children's [Israel's] bread, and to cast *it* to dogs [Gentiles]," she responded, "Truth, Lord: yet **the dogs eat of the crumbs which fall from their masters' table.**" Because she said this, Christ responded, "great is thy faith." And Mark 7:28 tells us, "*for this saying*" he healed her daughter.

SEARCH THE SCRIPTURES

1. *See also Matthew 4:17*	4. *John 1:49 & 20:31; Matt. 16:16; Lk.12:32*
2. *Romans 15:8*	5. *Matt. 5:19-20 & 8:4 & 23:1-3; Lk 5:14*
3. *Matthew 15:24*	*(See also pages 20 and 32.)*

THE SIGNS OF THE KINGDOM

During his earthly ministry, Jesus Christ worked miracles to validate that he was the Messiah, God in the flesh. His miracles gave the people a foretaste of the coming kingdom.

The two hallmark signs of the kingdom were casting out devils and healing the sick. These signs fill the gospels. Christ said, "… if I with the finger of God cast out devils, no doubt the kingdom of God is come upon you."[1]

In casting out devils, he was demonstrating his capacity to "bind the strong man" [Satan] and spoil his house [the house of Israel]. [2] He was demonstrating that he was the one who would rescue Israel from Satanic captivity.[3]

When asked, "Art thou he that should come…?" Christ answered by quoting a passage about the kingdom: "the blind receive their sight, and the lame walk, the lepers are cleansed, and the deaf hear, the dead are raised up. . . ."[4] In other words, He was fulfilling the prophecies of the coming Messiah and kingdom.

Christ's miracles were a demonstration that he was God in their midst and the kingdom was indeed "at hand."

SEARCH THE SCRIPTURES

1. *Luke 11:20*
2. *Matthew 12:29*
3. *Isaiah 49:24-25*
4. *Matthew 11:3-6 with Isaiah 35:5-6*

CHRIST TEACHES ABOUT THE KINGDOM

Christ's earthly ministry focused on the kingdom promised to Israel in the Old Testament. In what is called the "Sermon on the Mount," Christ taught about the nature of this kingdom and those who will enter it. He exalted the law because once the kingdom is established, the law will be magnified and enforced on earth.[1] The law will be written in redeemed Israel's hearts, and God will "cause you [Israel] to walk in my statutes."[2]

Jesus Christ also said, the meek "shall inherit **the earth**."[3] He taught Israel to pray, "**Thy kingdom come**. Thy will be done **in earth,** as it is in heaven."[4]

In the parables, he taught about different aspects of the kingdom. For example, in the parable in Luke 19:12-27, he taught that a nobleman (Jesus Christ) went "to a far country" (heaven) to "receive for himself a kingdom, and to return." (Note Daniel 7:13-14 and Revelation 21:2,10.) Upon his return, those who were faithful were given cities in the kingdom to rule over, as the faithful in Israel will be given in the kingdom.[5]

In the parable of the householder and his vineyard, Matthew 21:33-45, Christ reveals that the kingdom will be taken from the apostate religious leaders of Israel and given to a nation (singular — the believing remnant in Israel, "the little flock"[6]) bringing forth the fruits thereof. Note how Isaiah 5:1-7 explains this parable. Israel is the vineyard of God.

SEARCH THE SCRIPTURES

1. *Matthew 5:17-48 w/ Isaiah 42:21*
2. *Jeremiah 31:33; Ezekiel 36:27; Isa. 2:3*
3. *Matthew 5:5; Psalm 37:9-11*
4. *Matthew 6:10*
5. *Obadiah 19-21; Psalm 69:35-36; Isaiah 54:3; 61:4-7*
6. *Luke 12:32*

CHRIST PREPARES ISRAEL FOR THE TRIBULATION PRIOR TO THE KINGDOM

While on earth, Jesus Christ prepared his disciples for the coming of the tribulation period that will purge Israel prior to the kingdom (page 25). For example, he told them that when they see the abomination of desolation spoken of by Daniel, they must flee to the mountains.[1] He told them to take no thought for what they shall eat or drink because God will take care of them.[2] He told them to sell that they had[3] (which believers did in Acts 2-4).

All these instructions were given because during the tribulation they will have to flee from the antichrist.[4] In the mountains, God will provide miraculously for them[5] just as he did for their fathers in the wilderness with *daily manna* and quail (p. 20), and for Elijah when he fled from King Ahab.[6] That's why Christ told them to pray, "Give us this day our **daily bread.**"[7]

Christ further taught that after the tribulation, he would come with his angels to gather his elect (believers of Israel) into their land.[8]

But first, Matthew 13:41-42 says, "The Son of man shall send forth his angels, and they shall gather out of his kingdom all things that offend, and them which do iniquity; And shall cast them into a furnace of fire … Then shall the righteous shine forth as the sun in the kingdom of their Father."

Please also read Luke 17:34-37, which is often mistakenly taught to be the rapture of the church. Compare it with Psalm 37:9 and Revelation 19:17. Note that those who are "taken" are taken to judgment, not to heaven. Those who are left are left to inherit the kingdom on earth.

SEARCH THE SCRIPTURES

1. *Matthew 24:15-16*
2. *Matthew 6:31*
3. *Luke 12:33*
4. *Matthew 24:16*
5. *Revelation 12:13-17*
6. *Exodus 16:15 & I Kings 17:4-6*
7. *Matthew 6:11*
8. *Matthew 24:27-31 with Ezekiel 37:21-28*

CHRIST'S 12 APOSTLES PREACH: "THE KINGDOM OF GOD IS AT HAND"

In preparation for the kingdom, Christ chose 12 apostles. He told them, "…when the Son of man shall sit in the throne of his glory, ye also shall sit upon twelve thrones, judging the 12 tribes of Israel."[1] They were to be his cabinet, so to speak. He sent these 12 to preach *to Israel only*, "The kingdom of heaven is at hand."[2] He gave them the signs of the kingdom.[3]

Note that "the gospel of the kingdom" preached by Christ and his apostles is **not** the gospel we preach today. For one thing, those who believed the gospel were promised eternal life in the kingdom God will establish on this earth, not eternal life in heaven.

In addition, when the apostles preached "the gospel of the kingdom," *they did not preach the cross,* which is central to the gospel today. They did not yet understand that Christ would have to die and be raised. In fact, late in their ministry, when Christ began to tell them of his coming death, Peter responded by saying, "Be it far from thee, Lord: this shall **not** be unto thee."[4] Additionally the scriptures are careful to tell us the following:

> " . . . they **understood none** of these things: and this saying was **hid from them**, neither knew they the things which were spoken."[5]

Please carefully compare Luke 9:1-6 with Luke 18:32-34 and Matthew 10:5-8 with Matthew 16:21-22 & 17:22-23.

These passages make it clear that the apostles preached "the gospel of the kingdom" with power and signs to validate their message, yet they understood nothing about the cross. Their gospel was, "Repent for the kingdom of heaven is at hand" (Matthew 10:7)

SEARCH THE SCRIPTURES

1. *Matthew 19:28; Isaiah 1:26*
2. *Matthew 10:5-7*
3. *Matthew 10:8; Hebrews 2:3-4*
4. *Matthew 16:22*
5. *Luke 18:34*

ISRAEL REJECTS HER KING

The leaders of Israel rejected Christ and called for his crucifixion. They said, "We have no king but Caesar."[1] Jesus Christ went to the cross willingly, trusting the will of the Father.[2] God raised him from the dead after three days. *(These events were the fulfillment of Israel's Feast of Passover and Feast of Firstfruits, p. 21.)*

The risen Christ then appeared to the apostles and gave them the Holy Ghost so that they would have the authority and understanding to carry on his ministry after his ascension.[3]

Luke 24:45 says that Christ "opened their understanding ..." Acts 1:3 says that he spent 40 days with them, "speaking of the things **pertaining to the kingdom of God.**"

So, in Acts 1:6, the apostles ask, "Lord, wilt thou at this time restore again the **kingdom to Israel**?"

He told them that they "shall be witnesses unto me both in Jerusalem, and in all Judaea, and in Samaria [these areas comprise the land promised to Israel], and unto the uttermost part of the earth."[4] *(For more details about the "Great Commission," see pages 48 and 59.)* **But, Christ had told them that they will not have gone over all the cities of Israel before he would return.**[5]

This is because, under the prophesied plan, Israel as a nation had to be cleansed during the tribulation, then Christ would come and send redeemed Israel to the Gentiles as His "kingdom of priests."[6] So, the apostles remained in Jerusalem throughout the early Acts period, preaching **to the Jews** and proselytes, calling on them to repent and believe that Jesus was their promised Messiah.[7]

SEARCH THE SCRIPTURES

1. *John 19:15*
2. *Acts 2:23; Matt. 26:39; Isa. 50:5-9*
3. *John 20:21-23; 14:26; 16:13*
4. *Acts 1:8*
5. *Matt. 10:23*
6. *Exodus 19:5-6; Isaiah 61:6*
7. *Acts 2:10,14, 22-40; 3:12-25; 5:30-31; 8:1*

ISRAEL'S LAST CHANCE:
THE WITNESS OF THE HOLY GHOST

From the cross, Christ had prayed, *"Father, forgive them; for they know not what they do."*[1] After his ascension, he sent the Holy Ghost to fill the apostles and disciples with power from on high.[2] *(The fulfillment of the Jewish Feast of Pentecost [p. 21], which had "fully come.")*

So, in Acts 2-5, the Holy Ghost, through Peter, gave the men of Israel one last chance to repent of rejecting their Christ.

Peter says that Acts 2 is **"the last days"** prior to the kingdom, as prophesied by Joel.[3] *(It is NOT said to be the first days of the body of Christ.)* Pentecost was one of the three times each year when *Jewish* men from every nation came to Jerusalem. These *Jews* were Peter's audience. (See p. 21; Acts 2:10.)

The Holy Ghost, through Peter, indicted Israel for the rejection of their Messiah. He said that they "by wicked hands have crucified and slain" the "Prince of life."[4]

Peter tells them, "Repent, and **be baptized** every one of you in the name of Jesus Christ **for the remission of sins** . . . Save yourselves from this untoward generation."[5] (The "generation of vipers," the apostate leaders of Israel, see Matthew 23:33-37 and 3:7.)

Peter says, "Repent ... And he shall send Jesus Christ, which before was preached unto you: Whom the heaven must receive until the times of restitution of all things [the kingdom], which God hath spoken by the mouth of all his holy prophets since the world began."[6] He reminds them, "**Ye** are the children of the prophets, and of the covenant which God made with our fathers."[7] The apostles worked miracles to validate their message and enlighten Israel,[8] but most of the leaders refused to believe and persecuted the apostles.

SEARCH THE SCRIPTURES

1. *Luke 23:34*	5. *Acts 2:38-40*
2. *Luke 24:49; Acts 2:4*	6. *Acts 3:19-21*
3. *Acts 2:16-17; Joel 2:28-32*	7. *Acts 3:25*
4. *Acts 2:22-24; 3:15; 5:30*	8. *Acts 3:1-11; Hebrews 2:3-4*

THE FALL OF ISRAEL:
THE BLASPHEMY AGAINST THE HOLY GHOST

By this point, the leaders of Israel had *rejected God the Father* by rejecting the ministry of John the Baptist, "a man sent from God."[1]

They had *rejected God the Son* by calling for his crucifixion.

Now they were *rejecting God the Holy Ghost* by persecuting the apostles and disciples who were filled with and speaking by the Holy Ghost.[2] This "blasphemy against the Holy Ghost" Jesus Christ had said would not be forgiven.[3]

Their "blasphemy against the Holy Ghost" culminated with the stoning of Stephen, who was "full of the Holy Ghost" (Acts 7:55). As he was dying, he looked up into heaven and saw Jesus *standing*.[4]

Prophecy says that the ascended Christ was to *sit* at the Father's right hand *until he made his enemies his footstool*.[5] The fact that Stephen saw him *standing* indicates that Jesus Christ was ready to initiate the time of judgment.[6] He was ready to "open the book, and to loose the seven seals" that would begin the Great Tribulation. [7] And, indeed, the next prophesied event was the Great Tribulation, "the time of Jacob's trouble."[7]

Israel fell, and God's wrath was ready to be poured out.

SEARCH THE SCRIPTURES

1. *John 1:6*   4. *Acts 7:55*
2. *Acts 4:8; 7:55-60*
3. *Matthew 12:31-32*
4. *Acts 7:55*
5. *Psalm 110:1 & Acts 2:34-35*
6. *Isaiah 2:19,21 & 3:13; Psalm 7:6; 9:19; 68:1: 82:8*
7. *Revelation 5:5-6*
8. *Jeremiah 30:7*

MID-ACTS & PAUL'S EPISTLES
(ROMANS-PHILEMON)

PROPHECY

INTERRUPTED:

GOD'S PLAN FOR

THE HEAVENS

REVEALED

THE CHURCH, THE BODY OF
CHRIST AND "THE MYSTERY"

A NEW DISPENSATION:
"THE DISPENSATION OF THE GRACE OF GOD"

But God's wrath did not fall! The fulfillment of prophecy did not continue. Why? What happened?

When the leaders of Israel finalized their rejection of Christ by committing the unpardonable sin under the prophetic plan, rather than pouring out his wrath, God interrupted the prophetic plan and poured out his grace: "Where sin abounded, grace did much more abound"![1]

How did God do this? He reached down and saved the leader of the rebellion, Saul of Tarsus.[2] To Saul (the Apostle Paul), he began to reveal the plan he had "kept secret since the world began": *"the mystery."*[3] In so doing, God began "the dispensation of grace."[4]

Remember, when we discussed Lucifer's rebellion in heaven, we said that God had a plan to regain the heavens, but he kept it secret. With Israel's fall and the salvation of Saul, God began to reveal it. God put his prophesied plan to restore the earth through Israel on hold *temporarily*[5] and began to initiate his secret plan to restore the heavenly places through a new creature called "the body of Christ."

> Through Paul, God began to reveal that he would form a *new* agency—the Church, the Body of Christ—that will rule and reign with him in the heavenly places. This "new creature," called the "one new man," and its heavenly hope is the focus of what God calls "the mystery" that was hid in God, not revealed before it was made known through Paul.[6]

SEARCH THE SCRIPTURES

1. *Romans 5:20*
2. *Acts 9:1-6; 22:1-21; 26:1-8; I Timothy 1:12-16*
3. *Ephesians 3: 1-3, 5, 9 and Romans 16:25*
4. *Ephesians 3:2 and Colossians 1:25*
5. *Romans 11:11, 15, 25-32*
6. *Colossians 1:23-26; Ephesians 2: 12-16 and 3:1-3*

40

"THE REVELATION OF THE MYSTERY"

The Old Testament spoke about, and the gospels focused on, God's plan to reclaim *the earth* through the kingdom promised to Israel. This plan had been **spoken about "by the mouth of his holy prophets, which have been <u>since</u> the world began."**[1] In early Acts, Peter tells Israel, "all the prophets from Samuel and those that follow after, as many as **have spoken**, have likewise foretold of these days."[2]

In contrast, the Apostle Paul writes about God's plan to reclaim the *heavenly places* through the church, the body of Christ. He calls the things he speaks of **"the revelation of the mystery"** (Romans 16:25).

This is what he says in Ephesians 3:2-3: "If ye have heard of the dispensation of the grace of God which is **given me** to you-ward: How that **by revelation he made known unto me the mystery…**"[3]

Paul claims that the things he was sent to proclaim had been "**kept secret <u>since</u> the world began.**"[4] He said that his message "in other ages was **not made known** unto the sons of men"[5] but "from the beginning of the world hath been **hid in God.**"[6]

He said that God "**in due times** manifested his word through preaching, which is committed **unto me.**"[7]

Clearly God had new information to reveal through Paul. The *risen* Christ appeared to Paul several times to progressively reveal the things pertaining to this new dispensation.[8]

SEARCH THE SCRIPTURES

1. *Luke 1:70*
2. *Acts 3:24*
3. *See also Colossians 1:25-26*
4. *Romans 16:25*
5. *Ephesians 3:5*
6. *Ephesians 3:9*
7. *Titus 1:3*
8. *Acts 26:16; Gal. 1:11-12; 2 Corinthians 12:1*

"THROUGH THEIR FALL SALVATION IS COME UNTO THE GENTILES" [1]

So, what changed with the new dispensation?

The covenants and promises of the Old Testament foretold that the salvation of the Gentiles, and their subsequent blessings in the kingdom, would be through the *rise* of Israel.[2] Israel had been chosen by God to be a "kingdom of priests" and a "light to the Gentiles."[3] The gospels and early Acts focused on the fulfillment of these promises being "at hand."

However, today, in the dispensation of grace, Gentiles are not being blessed through the **RISE** of Israel as prophesied, but "rather through their **FALL** salvation is come unto the Gentiles."[1] Israel has been cast away (temporarily).[4]

Israel is now on the same level as the Gentiles, no longer in favored nation status. In Romans 11:25, Paul says, "… this mystery… blindness in part has happened to Israel, until the fullness of the Gentiles be come in." *This is a drastic change from the prophesied plan!*

THE FULFILLMENT OF PROPHECY HAS BEEN TEMPORARILY INTERRUPTED.

Jews & Gentiles on equal ground

SEARCH THE SCRIPTURES

1. *Romans 11:11*
2. *See pages 24-25.*
3. *Exodus 19:5-6; Isaiah 61:6-9; Isaiah 60*
4. *Romans 11:11,15*

A NEW CHURCH: "THE BODY OF CHRIST"

In time past, believers of Israel (and proselytes) were God's "church."[1] ("Church" simply means a called-out assembly.) They comprise the church that will inherit the kingdom of God *on earth*.[2]

According to Ephesians 2:11-12, "in time past" Gentiles, apart from Israel, were "without Christ, **being aliens from the commonwealth of Israel, and strangers from the covenants of promise,** having no hope, and without God in the world."

"**But now** in Christ Jesus ye who sometimes were far off are made nigh by the blood of Christ" (Ephesians 2:13). In Paul's epistles, God says he has "**broken down** the middle wall of partition *[page 18]* . . . to make in himself of twain [Jew and Gentile] **one new man** . . . that he might reconcile both unto God in **one body** [the body of Christ] by the cross."[3]

The church God is forming today is "the body of Christ."[4] It is a new body of believers not talked about in the Old Testament or the gospels. In the body of Christ there is no difference between Jew and Gentile.[5] Today *anyone* who believes the gospel of the grace of God (page 45) becomes part of the body of Christ, not Israel. Paul says, "For by one spirit are we all baptized into one body, whether we be Jews or Gentiles."[6]

> The body of Christ is separate and distinct from Israel, with its own purpose, calling, and hope.

SEARCH THE SCRIPTURES

1. *Matt. 18:16-18; Acts 2:47 & 7:38*
2. *Luke 12:32; See page 29.*
3. *Ephesians 2:14-16*
4. *1 Cor. 12:27; Eph. 1:22-23*
5. *Romans 10:12; Gal. 3:27-28*
6. *1 Corinthians 12:1*

A NEW APOSTLE

In the gospels, Christ chose 12 apostles to rule with him over the 12 tribes of Israel in his kingdom. When Judas fell, Matthias was chosen to replace him.[1] Their number was complete, so **Why Paul?**

Paul's ministry is separate from that of the 12. God used Paul to reveal "the dispensation of the grace of God" to the Gentiles.[2] Paul, in Romans 11:13, says, "I am the apostle of the Gentiles, I magnify mine office." The risen Lord appeared to Paul several times during his ministry and progressively revealed[3] the truths *specifically about and for the church of today, the body of Christ, in the dispensation of grace.* Note what he claims:

❖ "According to the grace of God which is given unto me, as a wise masterbuilder, **I** have laid the foundation . . . let every man take heed how he buildeth thereupon" (I Cor. 3:10).

❖ ". . . for his body's sake, which is **the church: Whereof I am made a minister, according to the dispensation of God which is given to me** for you ." (Col. 1:24-25. See also Eph. 3:1-3.).

❖ "Now to him that is of power to stablish you according to **my gospel**, and the preaching of Jesus Christ **according to the revelation of the mystery**, which was kept secret since the world began. . . "(Romans 16:25).

❖ "Be ye followers of **me** . . ." (I Corinthians 4:16 & 11:1).

❖ ". . . that **in me FIRST** . . . for a pattern to them which should hereafter believe on him to life everlasting" (I Timothy 1:16).

❖ ". . . For I neither received it of man, neither was I taught it, but **by the revelation of Jesus Christ.**" (Galatians 1:12)

SEARCH THE SCRIPTURES

1. *Matt 19:28; Isaiah 1:26; Acts 1:26*
2. *Ephesians 3:1-3*
3. *Acts 26:16; 2 Corinthians 12:1*

A NEW GOSPEL:
"THE GOSPEL OF THE GRACE OF GOD"

During his earthly ministry, Christ and his apostles preached "the gospel of the kingdom," the good news that the kingdom of God was "at hand." This message included the law (p. 32). In Acts, _believing_ Jews who were saved under the kingdom gospel rightly continued to keep the law (Acts 10:14 & 21:20).

But to the Apostle Paul, the _risen_ Christ gave what he calls "the gospel of the grace of God" (Acts 20:24). Through the Apostle Paul, Christ revealed "the end of the law" (Romans 10:4) and salvation by grace through faith _in the shed blood of Christ alone_, apart from the law and apart from works. In Romans 3:21-28 Paul says this:

> **"BUT NOW** the righteousness of God **without the law** is manifested . . . Being justified freely by his grace through the redemption that is in Christ Jesus: Whom God hath set forth _to be_ a propitiation **through faith in his blood** . . . a man is justified by faith **without the deeds of the law."**

It is in Paul's epistles that we read things like the following:

❖ ". . . for ye are not under the law, but under grace" (Romans 6:14).

❖ ". . .to him that **worketh not,** but believeth on him that justifieth the ungodly, his faith is counted for righteousness" (Romans 4:5).

❖ ". . . in him, not having mine own righteousness, which is of the law, but that which is through the faith of Christ, the righteousness which is of God by faith" (Philippians 3:9).

❖ "For **by grace** are ye saved through faith; and that not of yourselves: _it is_ the gift of God: **Not of works**..." (Ephesians 2:8-9).

❖ "Stand fast therefore in the liberty wherewith Christ hath made us free, and be not entangled again with the yoke of bondage" (Galatians 5:1).

"THE PREACHING OF THE CROSS"

While the Old Testament and the gospels did reveal that Christ would die and be raised for the sins of *his people* (Israel),[1] the shed blood of Christ was not at the heart of "the gospel of the kingdom" preached during the earthly ministry of Christ and early Acts. To "believe on Christ" at that time was to believe that he was the Son of God, the promised Christ and King of Israel.[2] As late as Luke 18:31-34, after extensively preaching *"the gospel of the kingdom,"* the apostles still did not understand that Christ would have to die. (See p. 34.) After his death, they did not preach the cross as good news, but as a wicked deed that Israel needed to repent of.[3]

This is because there are many things that the cross of Christ accomplished that God purposely kept hidden until he revealed them through Paul. He kept this "hidden wisdom" a secret so that Satan and his princes would not know it, **"for had they known *it*, they would not have crucified the Lord of glory."**[4] (See page 50.)

The "hidden wisdom" about the cross is at the heart of the gospel of the grace of God and the mystery revealed through Paul.

"The preaching of the cross," as Paul calls it, is what makes salvation by grace *through faith in the blood of Christ alone* possible. Paul says, ". . . unto us which are saved, it is the power of God."[5] The preaching of the cross begins with the good news that Christ "was delivered for our offenses, and was raised again for our justification,"[6] but it is so much more. It is *everything* that God is free to do because of the sacrifice of Christ. (*Please see page 47.*)

A critical fact to note: In Matthew 26:28, Christ says that his blood "is shed **for many**" (meaning Israel). But Paul declares that Christ "gave himself a ransom **for all**, to be testified **in due time**. **Whereunto I am ordained** a preacher, and an apostle" (I Tim 2:6-7).

SEARCH THE SCRIPTURES

1. *Isaiah 53:8,12; Acts 5:31*
2. *John 1:49; Matt. 16:16; John 20:30-31*
3. *Acts 2:22-24 and 32-38 (see p. 36)*
4. *1 Corinthians 2:7-8*
5. *Corinthians 1:18*
6. *Romans 4:25; 1 Cor. 15:3-4*

COMPLETE "IN CHRIST"

One of the most blessed truths we learn through "the preaching of the cross" is our completeness *in Christ.*[1] During this dispensation of grace, the moment a person places his faith in the shed blood of Christ *alone* for salvation, he is "baptized **into Jesus Christ**" by the Holy Spirit[2] — into his death, burial, and resurrection.[3] Believers are "sealed with that Holy Spirit of promise."[4]

In Christ, believers have complete forgiveness of all their sins and the imputed righteousness of God — the righteousness of God which is by faith of Jesus Christ.[5] We become "heirs of God, and joint-heirs with Christ,"[6] and nothing "shall be able to separate us from the love of God, which is **in Christ Jesus our Lord.**" [7]

This is a contrast to Israel's program in time past. Today, *in Christ*, among the many blessings we have, we also have spiritually what was required of Israel physically under the law:

- ❖ Israel had to continually offer blood sacrifices for sins; we now know we have total, complete forgiveness of all our sins — past, present, and future — by the blood of Christ.[8]

- ❖ Israel had to be physically circumcised; we are spiritually circumcised "with the circumcision made without hands . . . **by the circumcision of Christ.**"[9]

- ❖ Israel had to be physically baptized with water; we are "buried **with him in baptism**...through the faith of the operation of God"—a spiritual baptism into the death of Christ.[10]

SEARCH THE SCRIPTURES

1. *Colossians 2:10*
2. *Romans 6:3; I Cor. 12:13*
3. *Romans 6:3-8; Gal. 2:20*
4. *Ephesians 1:13-14*
5. *Romans 4:5 ,22-24; 2 Corinthians 5:21; Philippians 3:9; Ephesians 1:7*
6. *Romans 8:17*
7. *Romans 8:35-39*
8. *Colossians 2:13-14 & 1:14*; Romans 3:25; Eph. 1:7*
9. *Colossians 2:11*
10. *Colossians 2:12; Romans 6:3-12; I Corinthians 12:13; Galatians 3:27*

A NEW COMMISSION: "THE MINISTRY OF RECONCILIATION"

Prior to his ascension, Christ gave his apostles what has been called "The Great Commission." He instructed them that, beginning at Jerusalem, then Judea, then Samaria (the land areas promised to Israel), and finally all nations, they were to go and teach men "to observe all things whatsoever I have commanded you."[1] This would mean the truths about the kingdom being at hand. It would also include the law.[2] In this commission, Christ sent them to baptize *for the remission of sins*. He said, "He that believeth *and is baptized shall be saved*," and that is what was preached in early Acts.[3]

In contrast, Paul says, "Christ sent me **not to baptize**."[4] While Paul did baptize a few people prior to receiving the *full* revelation of the mystery, once that revelation was complete, he stopped baptizing. In his epistles we find that believers today have a spiritual baptism that has replaced water baptism.[5]

In addition, the Lord sent Paul to preach that, "Christ is the end of the law for righteousness to everyone that believeth,"[6] so that we are "not under the law, but under grace." (See page 45.)

It is clear that Paul is operating under a different commission from the twelve. Indeed, to the body of Christ, God has given a new commission, found in 2 Corinthians 5:16-21, called "the ministry of reconciliation." As "ambassadors for Christ" we are to proclaim to the world that "God was **in Christ**, reconciling the world unto himself, not imputing their trespasses unto them . . . For he [God] hath made him [Christ] *to be* sin for us, who knew no sin; that we might be made the righteousness of God **in him**."

SEARCH THE SCRIPTURES
1. *Matthew 28:19+; Mark 16:15+; Luke 24:46+; Acts 1:8*
2. *Matthew 28:20; 23:1-3; 5:17-19*
3. *Mark 16:16; Acts 2:38*
4. *I Corinthians 1:17*
5. *I Cor. 12:13; Colossians 2:10-12; Romans 6; Ephesians 4:5; Gal. 3:27*
6. *Romans 10:4*

A NEW HOPE: HEAVEN

Prior to the dispensation of grace, the hope of God's people was to be resurrected into a kingdom God will establish on this earth.[1] And, indeed, those who were saved in the Old Testament and under the kingdom gospel in Matthew though early Acts will be resurrected into that kingdom.

Christ will one day be king over the earth and redeemed Israel will be ruling with him over the Gentile nations.[2] He taught that he would go away **and return**.[3] He said, "the meek shall inherit **the earth**."[4] The book of Revelation looks forward to the coming of God's kingdom to this earth when new Jerusalem will descend from heaven **to the earth**.[5]

But in Paul's epistles the hope of the believer is a home **"eternal in the heavens."**[6] Members of the body of Christ will rule and reign with Christ **in the heavenly places**. In fact, Ephesians 2:6 says that God already sees us raised up together and seated together in heavenly places in Christ Jesus.

Philippians 3:20 also says that "our conversation is in heaven" and 1 Corinthians 6:3 says we shall judge angels. Clearly the realm of "the new creature," the body of Christ," is the heavenly places.

Remember, God's kingdom has two realms. He will rule both heaven and earth.

> The body of Christ is the agency God is going to use to reclaim the heavenly places that have been corrupted by the fallen angels.

SEARCH THE SCRIPTURES

1. See pages 24, 25, and 29
2. Zechariah 14:9; Jeremiah 23: 5-8 and 33:14-17; Psalm 47 and 72:8
3. John 14:3; Luke 19:12-15 w/ Dan 7:13-14
4. Matt. 5:5 & Psalm 37:9
5. Revelation 21:2, 10
6. 2 Corinthians 5:1

WHY KEPT SECRET?

Why did God keep the good news about this age of grace and the body of Christ a secret? I Corinthians 2:7-8 gives us the answer:

> "But we speak the wisdom of God in a mystery, *even* the hidden *wisdom*, which God ordained before the world unto our glory:
>
> Which none of the princes of this world knew: for **had they known** *it*, **they would not have crucified the Lord of glory.**"

When Satan moved the leaders of Israel to call for the crucifixion of Christ, he was gambling that this would require God to abandon his people forever;[1] thus, the earth would remain his. (See page 13.)

What he did not know was that not only was the death of Christ the means whereby God would later redeem his nation and take back the earth, it was also the means whereby he would form a new agency, the body of Christ, to reconcile the heavenly places unto Christ.

By keeping the dispensation of grace and the body of Christ (the "one new man") a secret, God was able to take Satan in his own craftiness.[2] Satan and his princes gambled for the earth, and in so doing they lost both the earth and the heavenly places in the ages to come. By Christ's victorious work on the cross, "he made a shew of them openly, triumphing over them in it."[3]

SEARCH THE SCRIPTURES

1. Satan did know that Christ was to die, but Israel was supposed to sacrifice "the lamb of God" by faith. (Compare Psalm 118:26-27 w/ Matthew 21:9.) Satan was able to move Israel to call for his death in unbelief, by "wicked hands" (Acts 2:23).
2. I Corinthians 3:19
3. Colossians 2:15

PAUL'S WARNING

Paul desired "to make all *men* see what *is* the fellowship of the mystery, which from the beginning of the world hath been hid in God."[1] But "the mystery" — the truths the risen Lord Jesus Christ revealed through Paul — is what Satan hates because it reveals how the cross was his defeat. It is the "preaching of Jesus Christ, according to the revelation of the mystery,"[2] that Satan tenaciously fights to keep hidden.[3]

Paul warned that after his departure, "grievous wolves" would enter in and "of your own selves shall men arise, speaking perverse things, to draw away disciples."[4]

Even before he died, Paul had to say, "all they which are in Asia be turned away *from me*."[5] The majority of the churches he had started had left his doctrine. Many, like the Galatians, returned to the law. (This is one reason that we cannot rely on "the church fathers" for our doctrine. We must rely on the word of God alone.)

Even to this day many still fail to see Paul's distinctive ministry and understand "the mystery" God revealed through him. This is sad because it is Paul's gospel and "the preaching of Jesus Christ according to the revelation of the mystery" that "stablishes" a believer today.

> "Now to him that is of power to stablish you according to my gospel, and the preaching of Jesus Christ, according to the revelation of the mystery, which was kept secret since the world began . . ."
>
> (Romans 16:25)

It is no wonder that the church is in such confusion today!

SEARCH THE SCRIPTURES

1. Ephesians 3:9
2. Romans 16:25
3. 2 Corinthians 4:3-4
4. Acts 20:29-30
5. 2 Timothy 1:15

SOLVING THE CONFUSION: THE GOSPEL

Failing to recognize the distinctiveness of "the revelation of the mystery" given to Paul by the *risen* Christ leads to confusion. For example, mixing the kingdom gospel with the gospel of the grace of God perverts the gospel for today. When Christ and the 12 preached the kingdom gospel, the law was still in effect. Christ said, "Whosoever shall do and teach the same [the law], shall be called great in the kingdom of heaven."[1] Also, Christ and the 12 commanded various works. For example, Christ said, "... if ye forgive men not their trespasses, neither will your Father forgive your trespasses,"[2] and "He that believeth *and is baptized* shall be saved."[3] Peter preached, "Repent and *be baptized . . . for the remission of sins.*"[4] These are NOT "the gospel of the grace of God."

In addition, Christians who try to apply verses given to Israel to themselves may question their eternal security. Consider these:

> "He that shall endure to the end, ... shall be saved" (Matt 24:13).

> "For it is impossible for those who were once enlightened, ... If they shall fall away, to renew them again unto repentance..." (Heb. 6:4-6).

These verses mean what they say for the time and situation in which they were intended. They apply during the "last days" of the prophetic program, which began in early Acts (note Acts 2:16-17) and will continue when this dispensation of grace is over and the Great Tribulation begins. They do not apply today. In this age of grace, *no works of any kind are required for salvation* and *all believers are eternally secure.* It is *through Paul* that God explains how we are justified apart from the law and works in this dispensation of grace:

> " . . . being *justified freely by his grace* through the redemption that is in Christ Jesus: Whom God hath set forth to be a propitiation *through faith in his blood . . .*" (Romans 3:24-25).

SEARCH THE SCRIPTURES

1. Matthew 5:17-20; See also Matt. 23:1-3; 8:4; Luke 5:14
2. Matthew 6:15
3. Mark 16:16
4. Acts 2:38

SOLVING CONFUSION: SIGNS AND WONDERS

Another area of confusion among Christians concerns signs, wonders, and miraculous healings. In the gospels and Acts, these were a foretaste of the kingdom and validated the message that the kingdom was then at hand.[1] However, today the kingdom is not at hand. Today, the outer man is not the focus of God's activity. Instead, God is doing something far more wonderful and eternal than temporary healing and outward signs: he is working in the inner man of the believer, strengthening him by his Spirit to be able to glorify Him in any circumstance.[2] Even Paul, who at the beginning of his ministry performed many signs and healings, was unable to do so by the end of his ministry.[3] But he said, "I have learned, in whatsoever state I am, *therewith* to be content"(Phil 4:11).

Today, believers are blessed with "all **spiritual** blessings in heavenly *places* **in Christ**."[4] We understand that "though our outward man perish, yet the inward man is renewed day by day."[5] In 2 Cor. 12:9-10, Paul explains this.

"And he said unto me, **My grace is sufficient for thee:** for my strength is made perfect in weakness. Most gladly therefore will I rather glory in my infirmities, that the power of Christ may rest upon me. Therefore I take pleasure in infirmities, in reproaches, in necessities, in persecutions, in distresses for Christ's sake: for when I am weak, then am I strong."

And God would have us, too, learn to rest in the sufficiency of his wonderful grace, no matter what our outward circumstances!

"For our light affliction, which is but for a moment, worketh for us a far more exceeding and eternal weight of glory, . . . for the things which are seen are temporal, but the things which are not seen are eternal" (2 Cor. 4:17-18).

SEARCH THE SCRIPTURES

1. Heb. 2:3-4; Matt. 11:3-6 w/ Isa. 35; Lk. 11:20
2. 2 Cor. 4:16-18; 2 Cor. 4:7-10; Phil. 4:11-13
3. 2 Cor. 12:8-10; 2 Tim. 4:20; 1 Tim. 5:23
4. Ephesians 1:3
5. 2 Cor. 4:16-18

SOLVING CONFUSION: THE WILL OF GOD

When the Bible is not rightly divided, understanding the will of God also becomes confusing. In time past, under the law, God gave Israel detailed instructions about every aspect of their lives. The law is likened to "tutors and governors"; Israel, under the law, is likened to children and servants.[1] When Israel disobeyed, they were chastised. When they obeyed, they were blessed. External signs told them whether or not they were in the will of God.[2]

Today, however, God deals with believers as adult sons who no longer need tutors and governors.[3] We do not need external signs to determine if we are in the will of God. God has given us the indwelling Holy Spirit and his complete Word to instruct us.[4] Walking in the will of God today is simply walking in line with what God is doing today—letting Christ *in you* live out of you, and letting his word effectually work in you as you believe and trust it.[5]

In some areas of life, God's Word gives specific instructions. When we obey these instructions by faith, we are doing the will of God. For example, husbands are instructed to love their wives; wives to submit to their husbands; and children to obey their parents.[6]

But there are many areas about which the Bible is silent. In these areas, God gives the believer, as an adult son, freedom to choose. *God does not reveal his will today by external signs. God is not giving extra-biblical revelations.* His word is complete, making "the man of God ... throughly furnished unto all good works."[7] We discern his will by "the renewing of [our] minds" in the Word of God.[8] If a decision is not contrary to sound doctrine for this dispensation of grace, a believer is free to make it without fear of being out of the will of God.

> Understanding how God is working today is liberating! We do not have to wonder what God is trying to tell us—we have his complete word!

SEARCH THE SCRIPTURES

1. Galatians 4:1-2	4. Rom. 8:14; Col. 3:16	7. 2 Tim 3:16-17
2. Leviticus 26	5. Gal. 2:20; 1 Thes. 2:13	8. Rom. 12:1-2
3. Galatians 4:4-7	6. Eph. 5:21-6:1	

END OF THE DISPENSATION OF GRACE

This age of grace will not last forever. It will end when Jesus Christ comes to take the members of the body of Christ—everyone saved during this dispensation of grace—to heaven, where they will rule over the angels and glorify God forever.[1] This event is often called the Rapture of the Church; however, the word "rapture" is not the Biblical term. I Thessalonians 4:17 says believers will be "caught up together with them [the dead in Christ] in the clouds, to meet the Lord in the air: and so shall we ever be with the Lord."

At this event, the members of the body of Christ will receive glorified bodies and be manifested to be "the sons of God." This is what the Bible calls "the adoption" of the body of Christ that we, and all of creation, are waiting for.[2]

The body of Christ will fill the heavenly places and rule and reign with Christ there forever. We will be "the fullness of him that filleth all in all."[3]

God will put *us* on display in the heavenly places for all of creation to see in order to show "the exceeding riches of his grace in *his* kindness toward us through Christ Jesus."[4]

This is God's "eternal purpose which he purposed in Christ Jesus our Lord"[5] for the church, the body of Christ.[6]

SEARCH THE SCRIPTURES

1. *1 Thessalonians 4:16-17; 1 Corinthians 6:3*
2. *Romans 8:19-23; Philippians 3:20-21 5.*
3. *Ephesians 1:23*
4. *Ephesians 2:6-7*
5. *Ephesians 3:11*
6. *Ephesians 3:20-21*

HEBREWS – REVELATION

PROPHECY

RESUMES

FULFILLMENT

PROPHETIC EVENTS TO COME

Much of prophecy has already been fulfilled literally by events recorded in the gospels and early Acts. However, much is still left to be fulfilled — most importantly the establishment of the kingdom promised to Israel. (See Romans 11:26-29: "**All Israel shall be saved: As it is written. . . . "**) The following passages make this clear.

❖**Luke 4:17-21**

Jesus Christ read a passage from the book Isaiah, closed the book, and said, "This day is this scripture fulfilled in your ears." Compare what he read to the passage in Isaiah 61:1-2 from which he quoted. You will discover that *he stopped reading right in the middle of a sentence!* He read, "The Spirit of the Lord *is* upon me, because he hath anointed me to preach the gospel . . . To preach the acceptable year of the Lord. And he closed the book." But the passage in Isaiah continues in the same sentence with ". . . and the day of vengeance of our God." He did not read that part of the sentence because the day of vengeance has not yet come.

❖**The Fulfillment of Israel's Feasts (p. 21, Exodus 23, Leviticus 23)**

The first group (the Feasts of Passover, Unleavened Bread, and Firstfruits) were fulfilled in the crucifixion, burial, and resurrection of Christ.

Fifty days later, the Feast of Harvest (also called Pentecost) was fulfilled on the day of Pentecost in Acts 2 ("the day of Pentecost was fully come" — Acts 2:1).

But the final group, the Feasts of Trumpets, the Day of Atonement, and the Feast of Tabernacles (picturing Israel's gathering into her land, national forgiveness, and entrance into the kingdom) have not yet been fulfilled.

❖**Daniel 2**

The vision in Daniel 2 pictures the rise and fall of great kingdoms that would rule over Israel. Babylon, Media-Persia, Greece, and Rome all rose and fell consecutively, but the last kingdom, the kingdom of the antichrist prior to the establishment of God's kingdom, has not yet risen.

PROPHETIC FULFILLMENT WILL RESUME

"The Dispensation of Grace" Interrupted Prophetic Fulfillment (Temporarily)

PROPHECY SPOKEN:	PROPHECY BEIGNS FULFILLMENT:	PROPHECY REJECTED: Israel's chance to repent and receive King & kingdom; Ministry of the Holy Ghost to Israel is rejected (Blasphemy of Holy Ghost)		THE MYSTERY Revealed through Paul	PROPHECY: RESUMES AND IS FULFILLED
The King and kingdom is promised to Israel	The kingdom is "at hand" Ministry of Christ to Israel		Transition period	PROPHECY INERRUPTED: The kingdom postponed while God forms THE BODY OF CHRIST "The Dispensation of Grace"	The Great Tribulation; then, The Kingdom established
Old Testament	Matthew-John	Acts 1-8	Acts 9-28	Romans-Philemon	Hebrews-Revelation

Once this dispensation of grace is over, God will resume the fulfillment of prophecy where it left off in mid-Acts—"the last days"[1] prior to the establishment of the kingdom. The next event in prophecy is "the time of Jacob's trouble,"[2] the Great Tribulation. The primary purpose of the tribulation is to be a "refiner's fire" and purge the rebels out of Israel, so that "the offering of Judah and Jerusalem [will] be pleasant to the Lord."[3]

The remnant (true believers out of the nation) will go through the fire but not be consumed as was symbolized by the burning bush in Exodus[4] and by Shadrach, Meshach, and Abed-nego.[5] Believers will know to flee to the mountains of the wilderness where God will provide for them, as he did for their fathers in the Exodus. (See pages 20 and 33.) In fact, Israel's Exodus from Egypt as they fled from Pharaoh is a marvelous picture of Israel's flight from the antichrist during the tribulation. God will again bare them on eagles' wings and provide their "daily bread." (Compare Exodus 15 (all) and 16:15-19 and 19:4-6 with Revelation 12:14-16.) God will work great signs and wonders through his two witnesses (Moses and Elijah) and 144,000 Israelites whom he will "seal."[6]

SEARCH THE SCRIPTURES

1 Acts 2:16-17; Hebrews 1:1-2
2 Jeremiah 30:7
3 Malachi 3:2-4; Ezek. 22:17-22
4 Exodus 3:2-3; Malachi 3:6; Isaiah 43:2
5 Daniel 3:19+
6 Revelation 11:3-7 & 7:4

DOCTRINE FOR THE "AGES TO COME"

After this dispensation of grace, people on earth will need instructions. When Christ was on earth, he taught as if there would be no interruption in the fulfillment of prophecy. Hence, his instructions will again apply when prophecy resumes.

For example, in Matthew 24:15-21, Christ says, "When ye therefore shall see the abomination of desolation, spoken of by Daniel the prophet, . . . let them which be in Judea flee into the mountains: ... for then shall be great tribulation ... ." (See also page 33.)

The details in the Great Commission at the end of the gospels and the beginning of Acts are also instructions that will be necessary once the fulfillment of the prophetic program resumes. Believers then will be empowered with miraculous signs to help them through the tribulation, as Mark 16:16-18 proclaims:

> "... **these signs shall follow** them that believe . . . cast out devils . . . speak with new tongues . . . take up serpents; . . . drink any deadly thing, it shall not hurt them. . . ."

During the tribulation, these signs will be necessary because plagues will be put upon the earth, such as serpents being used to kill men,[1] and waters being poisoned.[2] Also, Israel will need to preach to Jews of all languages, so they will need the gift of tongues, like in Acts 2:6. Then, following the tribulation Israel will become a "kingdom of priests" and will go into all the world and teach the Gentiles as commanded in Matthew 28:19.[3]

In addition, the entire last section of the Bible (Hebrews-Revelation) has "the last days" — the days leading to and including the establishment of the God's kingdom on earth — in view. (See p. 61)

SEARCH THE SCRIPTURES

1. *Revelation 6:8; Jeremiah 8:17 (serpents also symbolize Satan)*
2. *Revelation 8:11*
3. *Zechariah 8:23; Isaiah 61:6-9*

HEBREWS - REVELATION

The books of Hebrews-Revelation focus on and equip the believing remnant of Israel for the "last days" of the prophetic program.

> It is amazing to see that God's word is laid out in order just as it will work out in history.

Most of these final books were written during the early-Acts time period, before the prophetic fulfillment was interrupted. These books will again apply when prophecy resumes. Note a few of the many references in these books to the last days, the tribulation, and the 2nd coming of Christ:

Heb. 1:2	"in these last days"
Heb. 2:5	"the world to come"
James 5:8	"the coming of the Lord draweth nigh"
I Peter 1:6-13	"for a season . . . the trial of your faith . . . tried with fire . . . might be found unto praise and honour and glory at the appearing of Jesus Christ . . ."
I Peter 5:8	"... the devil, as a roaring lion, walketh about ..." *(See Revelation 12:12-13. Satan is cast to earth during the tribulation.)*
I John 2:18	" . . . it is the last time: and as you have heard that antichrist shall come . . . it is the last time."
Jude 14-15	" . . . the Lord cometh with ten thousands of his saints, To execute judgment . . ."
Rev. 1:9	" . . . your brother, and companion in tribulation and in the kingdom . . ."

ISRAEL WILL AGAIN BE GOD'S PEOPLE

When prophecy resumes, Israel and the earth will again be the focus of God's plans as he fulfills the covenants made with their fathers. (See **Romans 11:26-27**.)

❖ **Hebrews** reminds the *Hebrews* of the earthly ministry of Christ and of the witness of the Holy Ghost working in the apostles. It warns them not to neglect the salvation that was confirmed by them with signs and wonders.[1]

Hebrews also continually reminds them not to make the same mistake their fathers made with Moses when they did not enter their land because of unbelief.[2] It tells them that if they fall away, it will be impossible to renew them again unto repentance—it will be impossible for them to enter into the kingdom.[3] This is their last chance.

❖ **James** states quite plainly that he is writing to "the twelve tribes which are scattered abroad."[4] Remember, God had scattered Israel among the nations because of their disobedience and idolatry.[5]

❖ **Peter** also says he is writing to the "scattered."[6] He tells his audience they are "a royal priesthood" and an "holy nation" just as God said Israel would be.[7]

❖ **John** says he is "your brother, and companion in tribulation, and in the kingdom."[8]

Remember, *James, Peter, and John* agreed to confine their ministry *to the circumcision.*[9]

SEARCH THE SCRIPTURES

1. *Hebrews 2:3-4*	6. *I Peter 1:1*
2. *Hebrews 3:7-18*	7. *I Peter 2:9; Exodus 19:5-6*
3. *Hebrews 6:4-6*	8. *Revelation 1:9*
4. *James 1:1*	9. *Galatians 2:9*
5. *Lev. 26:33-39; Jer. 50:17; Ezek. 36:19*	

THE SECOND COMING OF CHRIST

At the end of the tribulation, Jesus Christ will mount his white horse and return to the earth with his angels to make war with his enemies and establish his kingdom. He will crush the antichrist and his armies in the great Battle of Armageddon. The beast and the false prophet will be cast into a lake of fire.[1] The Devil will be bound in the bottomless pit "that he should deceive the nations no more, till the thousand years should be fulfilled... ."[2] Unbelievers will be destroyed, and the believing remnant of Israel will be gathered to enter into the kingdom with their sins forever forgiven.[3] (*The fulfillment of the Feasts of Trumpets, Atonement, and Tabernacles. See p. 21.*)

In Matthew 25:31-46, Christ foretold of the judgment of the nations that will also occur at this time. Note that it is based on the Abrahamic Covenant (Genesis 12:1-3). Those who blessed Christ's "brethren" (Israel) during the tribulation are blessed and enter the kingdom; those who cursed his "brethren" (Israel) are cursed and cast into everlasting fire.

Believers who died with the hope of the kingdom (the Old Testament saints and believers during the gospels and early Acts period) will be resurrected in glorified bodies to enter the kingdom on earth.[4]

SEARCH THE SCRIPTURES

1. *Revelation 19:11-21*
2. *Revelation 20:1-3*
3. *Matthew 13:40-43; 24:27-31; Ezek. 36:25-28; 37:21-28; Psa. 37:9; Isaiah 11:11-12*
4. *Matthew 8:11 & 19:28-29*

THE 1000 YEAR REIGN OF CHRIST

After the tribulation and second coming, the 1000 year reign of Christ will begin. Satan will be bound in the bottomless pit.[1] Christ will be king over all the earth, ruling from Jerusalem. He will rule with perfect righteousness.[2]

The 12 apostles will sit on twelve thrones judging the 12 tribes of Israel.[3] Israel will finally be gathered and possess the land promised to Abraham, Isaac, and Jacob.[4] They will be under the new covenant and have the law written upon their hearts. God will do in them what they could not do in their own strength—keep the law.[5] The standards Christ taught in Matthew 5 when he magnified the law will be upheld.

Israel will be a light to the Gentiles—the kingdom of priests and ministers of God—that God created them to be.[6] Gentiles who want to be blessed will have to follow the law, keep the feasts, bless Israel, and seek the Lord in Jerusalem.[7]

During this time, the curse will be removed from the earth. The land of Israel will be like the Garden of Eden. The blind will see, the deaf shall hear, the lame walk, the dumb sing, the parched ground shall become a pool, the wolf shall dwell with the lamb... [8]

SEARCH THE SCRIPTURES

1. *Revelation 20:2-3*
2. *Zechariah 8:3 & 14:9; Isa. 9:6-7 & 11:4-5; Jer. 23:5 & 33:14-16*
3. *Matt. 19:28; Isaiah 1:26*
4. *Jeremiah 23:3-8; Ezekiel 37:21-28 & 20:40-42*
5. *Jeremiah 31:31-38; Ezekiel 36:22-29*
6. *Isaiah 61:6-9; Isaiah 60: 2-3, 14*
7. *Isaiah 2:2-4; Zech. 8:21-23 & 14:16-18; Isa. 60:3,5,12-16; Matt. 5:19-20*
8. *Ezekiel 36:34-35; Isaiah 35; Isaiah 11:6-7*

THE NEW HEAVEN & NEW EARTH:
"THE DISPENSATION OF THE FULLNESS OF TIMES"

At the end of the 1000 years, Satan will be loosed for a season. He will again deceive the nations.[1] There will be one final battle between the Lord and Satan and his followers. The Lord will be victorious. The Lord's enemies will be devoured by a great fire out of heaven, and Satan will be cast into the lake of fire forever. [2]

After this, the "great white throne" of judgment will occur. This is the final judgment of all unbelievers. They will be judged according to what is written in "the books" (the Bible) and the book of life. Ultimately, they are cast into the lake of fire with death and hell.[3]

There will be "a new heaven and a new earth."[4] The Body of Christ will have already been ruling with Christ in heaven. The holy city, the new Jerusalem, will descend from God out of heaven. It will have 12 gates with *the names of the 12 tribes of Israel and 12 foundations with the names of the 12 apostles.*[5] (Note that the 12 would not include Paul.) God, in the person of Jesus Christ, will rule the earth from new Jerusalem through redeemed Israel forever.

Thus, "the dispensation of the fullness of times" will begin (Eph. 1:10). Jesus Christ will be "the blessed and only Potentate, the King of kings, and Lord of lords"[6] over all of creation, both in heaven and earth. Redeemed Israel will be ruling with Christ on earth; the body of Christ will be ruling with him in the heavenly places.

> **All things will be "gathered together in one . . . IN CHRIST, both which are in heaven and which are on earth; even in him."** (Ephesians. 1:10)

SEARCH THE SCRIPTURES

1. *Revelation 20: 3,7*
2. *Revelation 20:9-10*
3. *Revelation 20:11-15*
4. *Revelation 21:1*
5. *Revelation. 21:2,10-14*
6. *1 Timothy 6:15*

"Thou art worthy, O Lord, to receive glory and honour and power: for thou hast created all things, and for thy pleasure they are and were created."

-Revelation 4:11

APPENDIX
The Most Important Division in the Bible:

PROPHECY vs MYSTERY

Since Lucifer's fall, there has been rebellion in both realms of God's kingdom: heaven and earth. The Bible reveals God's two-fold plan to end that rebellion. It is His purpose to reconcile all things, both *in heaven and on earth,* to the headship of the Lord Jesus Christ in "a *new heaven* and a *new earth*" (Ephesians 1:10; Revelation 21:1).

THE EARTH: THE PROPHETIC PROGRAM

The prophetic program is God's purpose to establish a literal, physical, eternal "kingdom of heaven" on this earth, with Jesus Christ ruling from David's throne over redeemed Israel, who will be His kings and priests on the earth to rule over and minister to the Gentile nations.

This is the focus of the Old Testament, the gospels, and the books of Hebrews-Revelation.

HEAVENLY PLACES: "THE MYSTERY" PROGRAM

"The mystery" (Colossians 1:26; Ephesians 3:2-3) is God's purpose to form a spiritual body of believers called "the body of Christ" (a "new creature") who will be perfectly "conformed to the image of His Son" and who will rule with Him in the heavenly places over the angels for eternity.

It is called God's "hidden wisdom" because it was not spoken about nor written about until God revealed it to and through the Apostle Paul; thus, it is found only in Paul's epistles, *Romans through Philemon.*

"RIGHTLY DIVIDING THE WORD OF TRUTH" (2 Timothy 2:15)

All the Bible is **for us,** but it is not all **to us,** nor is it all about us. It is vital to know where **you** are in the outworking of God's purposes. Today, we live during "the dispensation of grace," during God's "mystery" program (Eph. 3:1-3). The fulfillment of the prophetic program has been interrupted temporarily (Romans 11:25-27).

PROPHECY
God's purpose "**FROM THE FOUNDATION OF THE WORLD**"   *Matt. 25:34*
"**SPOKEN ABOUT** since the world began"   *Luke 1:68-70; Acts 3:21-24*
ISRAEL is God's chosen nation   *Exo. 19:5-6; Deut. 7:6; Matt. 10:5-10 & 15:24; Rom. 9:4-5; I Peter 2:9*
Eternal home of believers is the **EARTH**   *Deut. 11:21; Psalm 37:9-11; Isa. 11:9; Matt. 5:5; 6:10; Acts 3:19-25*
Jesus Christ to be **KING OF ISRAEL** and earth, ruling from David's throne   *Psa. 47; Isa. 9:6-7; Jer. 23:5-6; Zech. 14:9; Matt. 2:2; John 1:49;*   *Luke 1:31-33 and 67-79; Acts 2:30*
The central gospel is **"THE GOSPEL OF THE KINGDOM"**   *Matt. 3:2; 4:17,23; 24:14; Mark 1:14-15; John 1:49*
Israel is under the **LAW** given through **MOSES**   *Matt. 5:18-19; Matt. 23:1-3; Acts 21:20-21*   **Faith + works** *Matt.5:21-48; John 15:2; Acts 10:35; **James 2:24***   **Forgiveness conditional and can be lost**   *Matt. 6:14-15; **Matt. 18:23-35**; Matt. 24:13; Hebrews 6:4-6*
MIRACLES & HEALINGS validate the "gospel of the kingdom"   *Matt. 9:35; 11:2-5; 12:28-30; Matt. 10:5-9; Mark 16: 17; Luke 9:1-2;*   *Luke 11:20; Hebrews 2:3-5*
Gentiles will be blessed through the **RISE of Israel**   *Genesis 12:1-3; Isa 61:6-9; Isa. 60:11-14; Zech. 8:22-23*
Israel to be purged through the **"GREAT TRIBULATION"** prior to kingdom being established on earth; unbelievers shall be "taken" out   *Jer. 30:7; Mal. 3:2-4; Zech. 13:8-9; Ezek. 20:37-42 & 22:18-22;*   *Matt. 24:15-21 & 29-31; Matt. 13:40-43; Luke 17:34-37*
Physical **CIRCUMCISION and BAPTISM** required   *Circumcision: Gen. 17: 9-14; Luke 2:21*   *Baptism: Exo. 29:4; Mark 1:4; Mark 16:16; Luke 7: 29-30; Acts 2:38*
PETER is the chief apostle   *Matt. 16:18; Acts 1:15 & 2:14*

MYSTERY
God's purpose "**FROM <u>BEFORE</u> THE FOUNDATION OF THE WORLD**"   *Eph. 1:4; 3:10-11; 1 Corinthians 2:7*
"**KEPT SECRET**" and "hid in God" since the world began   *Romans 16:25; Eph. 3:9; Col. 1:26; I Cor. 2:7-8*
The **BODY OF CHRIST** is being formed in which there is **NO DIFFERENCE** between Jew and Gentile   *Romans 10:12; 1 Cor. 12:13; Gal. 3: 26-28; Eph. 2:14-15*
Eternal home of believers is the **HEAVENLY PLACES**   *Eph. 2:6; Philippians 3:20; Col. 3:1-4; 2 Cor. 5:1*
Jesus Christ is the **HEAD OF THE BODY OF CHRIST**   *Eph. 1:22-23; Col 1:18*
The central gospel is "**THE GOSPEL OF THE GRACE OF GOD**"   *Acts 20:24; Romans 3:21, 24-28; Ephesians 2:8-9; Ephesians 3:2*
Body of Christ is under **GRACE** revealed through **PAUL**   *Eph. 3:1-3 & 8-9; Romans 6:14; Gal. 2:16,21 & 5:1-4; Col 1:25; I Cor. 4:16-17*   **Faith alone, "not of works" Romans 4:5**; *Eph. 2:8-9; Titus 3:5-7*   **Forgiveness unconditional/ Believers are eternally secure**   *Ephesians 1:7; Ephesians 1: 13-14; Ephesians 4:32; Col. 2:13*
God's **GRACE IS SUFFIECIENT;**   Focus of God's activity is the **INNER MAN** to give peace *through* suffering   *2 Cor. 12:8-10; 2 Cor. 4: 8-12; 17-18; Phil. 4:11-13 & 1:29; 2 Tim 4:20*
Gentiles are blessed through the **FALL of Israel**   *Acts 28:27-28; Romans 11:11,15, 25*
Body of Christ will be "**DELIVERED... FROM THE WRATH TO COME**" (Pre-tribulation rapture)   *I Thes. 1:10 & 5:9; I Thes. 4:16-18; I Corinthians 15:51-57*
SPIRITUAL CIRCUMCISION and BAPTISM "in Christ ... without hands"   *Circumcision: Galatians 5:2; Col. 2:10-14*   *Baptism: Romans 6: 1-5; I Cor. 12:13; Col. 2:10-13; Gal. 3:26-28*   Note: Spiritual baptism is the "**ONE baptism**" for Body of Christ ***Eph. 4:5***
PAUL is the chief apostle   *Romans 11:13; I Cor. 3:10; Eph. 3:1-2; Col. 1:25-26; I Tim. 1:16; 1 Tim. 2:5-7*

Made in the USA
Las Vegas, NV
12 May 2024

89853502R00042